Inner Beauty of Nature

X-RAY PHOTOGRAPHY

Best *[signature]*

05/13/2014

BERT MYERS

Inner Beauty of Nature

X-RAY PHOTOGRAPHY

2007

Copyright 2007 by Bert Myers Fine Art Photography
37 Lark St.
New Orleans, LA 70124-4524
Phone and FAX 504 282 4022
Email: mbmyers@bellsouth.net
www.bmyersphoto.com

ISBN # 978-0-9792206-0-9

PUBLISHED BY
APPLEJACK ART PARTNERS
P.O. BOX 1528
HISTORIC ROUTE 7A
SUNDERLAND, VERMONT 05250
PHONE: (802) 362-3662

Printed and bound in the United States of America

Acknowledgments

When I first began x-raying shells I borrowed them from friends or bought them in shell shops in Northwestern Florida, and used the names given to me by the sellers. When I decided to produce a book I knew I needed the correct common and scientific names of the shells. Initial identification of many of the shells were made by Karen Kandyl, Ph.D., Professor of Biology at the University of New Orleans. She put me in contact with Ryan Taylor of Lafayette, LA who made further identifications and loaned me many shells to x-ray and photograph.

Later, I joined the Louisiana Malacology Society, and all of their members have been helpful in identifying and lending me shells. I especially want to thank Emelio Garcia, emeritus Professor of Romance Languages at Southeastern University in Lafayette LA. He has a personal collection of over 100,00 shells and has published many articles in peer reviewed scientific journals. He is a world expert on molluscs and land snails; he made the final identifications of most of the shells in this book and also loaned me numerous rare shells from his personal collection so I could photograph and x-ray them.

Other members of the club who loaned me shells include Cecil Bankston, M.D., Harriet Cole, Juanita and Nice Cacciopa of Baton Rouge, LA and Rusty Williams of Slidell, LA.

The frog shell was given to me by Kelsey Coste, great granddaughter of Irwin Buffet, friend and photographer who taught me much about conventional darkroom techniques, matting and mounting.

Jerry McClure of New Orleans loaned me several very old shells he found on the beach at Lake Pontchartrain in New Orleans.

Gene Usdin, M.D. of New Orleans supplied me with several cowery shells.

Nathan Kern, M.D. retired pediatrician and self-taught PhotoShop master, was my consultant for all things relating to digital photography.

All of the roses imaged in this book were supplied by Salem Sayegh, M.D. a former president of the American Rose Society.

Dr. Enrique Palacios, Director of Radiology at the VAMC New Orleans, allowed me to use their Fuji digital recording equipment to make images with my Faxiton x-ray machine. James Washington, Diagnostic supervisor and, Robert Wynn, chief technologist, were helpful in capturing the images and putting them on a CD.

Design and layout of the book was done by Michael Ledet, 19056 Magnolia Banks West, Hammond, LA 70401.

Final digital processing was done by PM Graphics, LLC, 605 Elysian Fields, New Orleans, LA 70117.

Dr. Donald Bradburn, Chief of Pathology at Touro Infirmary in New Orleans, who allowed me to use their Faxitron, after the one I had at the VA hospital was rendered unusable by hurricane KATRINA.

My wife, Joel Grossman Myers, was very helpful in editing the text and selecting the images to be included in this book. She also supplied me with innumerable flowers from her beautiful gardens.

Rose Blossom #1

TABLE OF CONTENTS

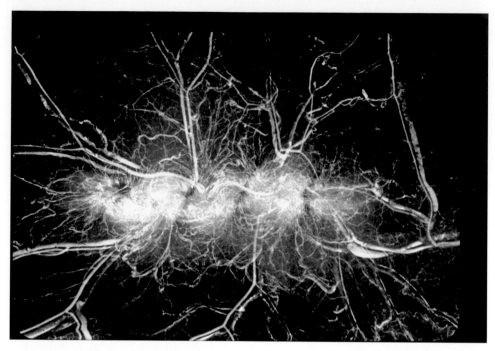

Anterior-posterior view of 10 day old wound

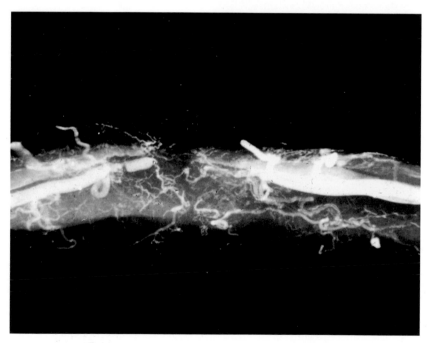

Cross section of 10 day old wound

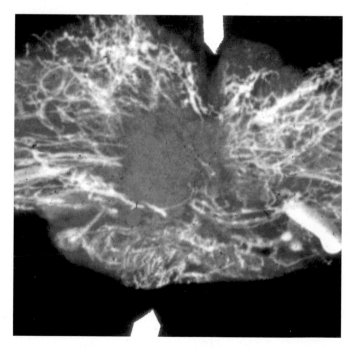

Cross section of 14 day wound showing a devascularized area from a tight suture

HISTORY OF X-RAY ART

X-rays were discovered by Wilhelm Roentgen in 1895, and their usefulness in medicine was immediately recognized worldwide. Within two years there was a New York Radiology Soceity, and with the discovery of better and safer equipment and now computer augmentation, the field has expanded logarithmically, even as non-x-ray imaging devices (ultrasound and magnetic resonance) became available.

The first published x-ray of a leaf was by Goby[1], a French scientist, in 1913. Hall Edward[2] in 1914 was the first to image a flower, and Engelbrecht[3] entered the field in 1931. It was Dain Tasker[4,5], a California physician radiologist, however, who popularized the technique. He had gallery shows in the 1930's, and a large number of his images can be seen in a recently published book[6].

In the 1920's, Man Ray, an American artist and photographer made images he called Rayographs. They were photograms, made by shining white light onto objects placed on light sensitive photo paper. The backgrounds were black, and the some of the objects translucent, so they looked like x-rays, and some consider him to be a pioneer in x-ray art, but that is not true. According to Timothy Baum[7] of the Man Ray Trust, Ray never used x-ray or other ionizing radiation to make images.

Beginning in 1960 Albert G. Richards[8], now Emeritus professor of Dentistry at Univ. of Michigan School of Dentistry began making x-ray images of flowers, and a large number of them can be seen in his book[9], published in 1990.

In 1963 Sherwood and Seemann[10] of the Kodak Research Laboratory published an article describing the technique of floral radiography.

William A. Conklin of Orangeburg, South Carolina, started making x-ray images of sea shells in the 1970's and his first show was in 1978 at The Museum of Natural History of the Smithsonian Institute Washington, D.C. His work can be seen in a book published in 1995[11].

My involvement began in the 1970's when as an academic surgeon at LSUMC I began studying the vascularization of the healing wound, using an x-ray technique called microangiography. To pursue this work I secured an NIH grant which allowed me to purchase a precision x-ray machine (Faxitron). My early images of blood vessels growing into tissue[12] looked like abstract paintings – see facing page, and unaware of the work above, I began to make x-ray images of flowers and shells, incorrectly thinking I was the first in the world to do so. There is an old saying in academic surgery that **"if you think you have discovered a new procedure (operation), all it means is that you have not read the German literature". In this case it was the French!**
After I had worked out some of the technical difficulties in x-ray photography as art and to encourage others to get into the field, I published details of the technique in 1983[13], and Steve Meyers[18] used the article to begin his work.

Merrill Raikes has an excellent review of the history of x-ray art on his WEB page[23].

In 2006 other practitioners of x-ray art that I am aware of are William Conklin[11], Don Dudenbostel[14], George Green[15], Albert Koetsier[16], Judith McMillan[17], Steve Meyers[18], Sonny Randon[22], Albert Richards[9], and Merrill C. Raikes[19] in the USA, and Nick Veasey[20] and Hugh Turvey [21] in the United Kingdom. Examples of their work and contact information can be found in the final section of this book.

References
1. P. Goby, la microradiographie et ses applications a l'anatomie vegetale. Bull. Soc. Franc Photogr 4:310-312 1913
2. J. Hall-Edwards, The Radiography of Flowers, Arch Roentgen Ray 19:30-31 1914
3. Hazel Engelbrecht, Science News Letter, October 10, 1931
4. D. Tasker, U.S. Camera, October 1939
5. D. Tasker, X-ray Goes Pictorial, Popular Photography 10:78-79 March 1942
6. Dr. Dain L. Tasker, ISBN 0-9703983-0-1 published by Stinehour Press © 2000 1021 Lancaster Road, Lunenburg, Vermont 05906
7. Timothy Baum, Personal Communication 7/18/2003
8 A.G. Richards, Floral radiography is my hobby Michigan Botanist 2:3-6 1963
9. The Secret Garden by Albert G. Richards ISBN 0-9628791-0-X Almar Company P.O. Box 15174, Ann Arbor, Mich 48104
10. H.E. Sherwood and Seeman, The Radiography of Flowers, Medical Radiology and Photography, 39:49-51 1963
11. Inner Dimensions The Radiographic World of William Conklin ISBN 1-56796-063-4 WRS Publishing Co., 701 N. New Road, Waco, TX 76710
12. M.B. Myers and G.Cherry, Blood Supply of Healing Wounds: functional and angiographic Archives of Surgery 62:49-52 1971
13. B. Myers, Radiography for Arts Sake, Applied Radiology, May 1983
14. Don Dudenbostel http://www.x-rayarts.com/
15. George Green, http://crowncity.com/shellfish/xraygast.htm
16. Albert Koetsier's work is visible at, http://www.beyondlight.com/
17. Judith McMillan, http://www.judithkmcmillan.com/
18. Steve Meyers' images can be seen at, http://www.xray-art.com
19. Merrill Raikes, M.D., P.O. Box 610 Conway, MA 01341 Phone 413.625.8352
20. Nick Veasey, http://www.nickveasey.com/
21. Hugh Turvey < http://www.gustoimages.com/>
22. Sonny Randon Studio http://www.sonnyrandon.com/
23. Raikes, M. http://radiographics.rsnajnls.org/cgi/content/full/23/5/1149#REF3

TECHNIQUE OF
MAKING ART ROENTGENOGRAMS

*T*o make a radiograph one must expose the object to penetrating irradiation (very short electromagnetic waves naturally produced in the nuclei of radioactive elements or in man-made tubes by hurling electrons at metal targets, generally tungsten or molybdenum). The radiation that passes through the object is recorded either on a gelatin silver emulsion or more recently a digital screen (CCD, CMOS, Foveon chip, etc.).

FINDING A SUITABLE X-RAY MACHINE

To make radiographs, almost any source of irradiation will do, but to image less dense objects like flowers, one will need a machine capable of producing "soft" x-rays—those in the 10-40 Kilovolt range. A small focal spot and a long tube to film distance will improve sharpness and depth of field in the image. Any x-ray machine used on humans—even dental units—will do for hard objects such as shells—but for "soft" objects such as flowers one will need one with a beryllium window. The ideal one produces both soft and hard x-rays; the one I use is called a Faxitron, and is completely safe for the operator, as the x-ray beam will not go on until the heavily lead lined cabinet is fully closed—NO STRAY IRRADIATION ESCAPES THE UNIT!!!

Such machines are found in most hospital operating room pathology suites—not the radiology department. The machines are used for specimen radiography, mainly of breast biopsies. They are generally used by the hospital staff during working days, and should be available for use for art on nights and weekends. When hurricane KATRINA flooded most of New Orleans, the hospital my unit was housed in was forced to close. Fortunately I was able to purchase a used one (the exact same model I had) for $900 on eBay.com.

CONVENTIONAL FILMS

The following discussion is about conventional films and chemical development. In all imaging fields there is a rapid world wide shift from film to digital, and manufacturers in the future will make less and less film.

Virtually any film will do, but for maximum sharpness a fine grain one should be used. In general films made for medical radiography are not satisfactory (to increase sensitivity and minimize the x-ray exposure to the patient there is emulsion on both sides of the film base and that leads to decreased sharpness). One exception is Kodak's Min R 2000 which is a fine grained film coated on only one side. For most images, that is my choice in 2006. The only disadvantages to the film are that it is available in only two sizes (18 X 24 and 24 X 30 cm), and it is more expensive than slower films. Also excellent, but much slower is Kodak's Kodalith film. In 2006 it was not easily available in sizes larger than 4" X 5". Also satisfactory is a special film made by Kodak for EXPEDX (a supplier to the printing industry) called Colorlok. It is available in sizes up to 12" X 18", but only on thin base, so it cannot be used in the automatic processors, as it will jam the rollers, but can be cut into smaller sizes under a red safelight.

One can develop the thicker films in automatic processors such as the X-O-Mat, but in my experience scratches sometimes result. I prefer tray or motorized drum development using Kodak's D19 developer diluted 1:1. Using trays, to insure even backgrounds, the film should be presoaked in water for 30 sec before development. If streaks appear in the background of the tray developed films, the more constant agitation of the drum will usually eliminate them. Streaks are more of a problem with images shot at low KV, and thus are more often seen in floral imaging than in those of shells and other "hard" objects.

CASSETTES

Due to their thickness conventional medical x-ray cassettes are not ideal, and it is better to wrap the film in home-made light proof envelopes made from the black plastic bags photographic film and paper comes in.

CONTRAST CONTROL

Contrast control is as much a problem in radiography as in general photography, as different parts of the object are more or less penetrable to the radiation. To achieve maximum detail in all parts of the object, as low a Kvp as possible should be used. With shells I usually start with 40 Kv, run test strips and work up to 130, the maximum output of my machine. In the Faxitron I have the mamp is permanently set at 3, so the only other variable is time. Most flowers will yield good images at 10-30 Kvp. Blossoms with waxy petals (such as lilies) can be imaged at 40 Kvp, in the range of a mammography machine. Exposure times will vary with the film and tube to film distance, and at 3 feet it is 1-5 minutes for Kodalith film. Test exposures can be made on photo paper, such as Kodak Polymax, which has about the same speed to x-ray as Kodalith film. If one does not have a darkroom near the x-ray machine, one can use 4" X 5" Polaroid B + W sheet film to determine the KV needed. It has about the same sensitivity to x-ray as Kodalith, which is 15 X slower than Min R. When using the Polaroid film, one must remember that it is a reversal process, and the paper image is positive. Judging exposure is reversed. If the print is too dark, one needs more exposure or higher KV, not less.

Due to the "heel effect" of all x-ray beams, the background will not be even, and will appear as a gradient with fall off on one side. Some x-ray artists like this, but I prefer an even background, somewhat achievable by only using the far left portion of the beam.

The first image, whether on film or opaque paper will be a negative, in that the background will be black and the densest part of the object will be the lightest. The x-ray negatives can be used either by contact printing or in an enlarger to make positives, which have a dark image on a white background. Using conventional film darkroom methods, if one wishes the final image to be negative, the original negative must be reversed. This can be done by copying it onto a new piece of film, either by contact printing, or in a camera. Such copying inevitably leads to some loss of sharpness, so if one wants negative images, it is much better to digitize them with a scanner, and then do the reversal in an editing program such as PhotoShop.

The original x-ray image will be the same size as the object, and can be enlarged or manipulated either optically or digitally. If one has access to a transparency scanner, the original negative can be scanned (preferably at least 300 dpi resolution) and the digital file opened in a graphics program such as PhotoShop. Rarely, some x-rays will have such high contrast that it is necessary to make the first positive print in an enlarger on gelatin silver paper, flashing the paper or dodging and burning parts of the image to achieve the balance desired. That positive image can then be scanned in a flat bed scanner, and further prints or manipulations made in an editing program.

SPECIMEN MANAGEMENT

Since exposures are long, the specimens cannot move during the exposure. All animals need to be dead, and round shells, which may roll off the film when the heavy Faxitron door is closed, need to be fixed in position. In such cases the shell can be attached to the film cassette with a small amount of adhesive such as two sided Scotch tape or Blue Tac. If the specimen—plant or animal—needs accurate positioning, it can be pinned to a piece of Styrofoam which is placed in contact with the film. If the Kvp is 40 or more, the Styrofoam itself will not show in the negative, and the pin or adhesive images can be removed in PhotoShop.

DIGITAL IMAGING

I have minimal experience with direct digital imaging. The Fuji recording plate is much faster than any x-ray film and is very fine grained. It is about 25 X faster than Kodalith and twice as fast as Min R. The digital image has a much broader contrast range than the film one. The main problem with digital capture is that the image is recorded in DICOM, a format widely used for medical imaging, but not compatible with most editing applications. To open in PhotoShop, one must use a graphic converter program (a good one is available at www. Lemkesoft.com) to change it to a TIFF or JPEG file. Once opened it has high resolution and seems to have more contrast range than film.

CONCLUSION

Part of the fun and excitement of making radiographs is its total unpredictability. Beautiful flowers can produce uninteresting images and an unexciting object fascinating ones. An example of that is the leaf of the rice paper plant (page 77). The plant is often considered a nuisance one, as its leaves can get huge, and it propagates widely. It can take over a garden, and its powdery shedding causes rashes and other allergies in some people.

THE NEGATIVE VERSUS POSITIVE DEBATE AND OTHER IMAGE MANIPULATIONS

The original image produced by x-ray or other ionizing radiation, whether on film (transparent) or paper (opaque) is always a negative one–the background is black and the densest parts of the object are the lightest. Traditionally physicians are used to looking at negative transparencies, and many people think that is the way an x-ray should look. Recently, however, with the advent of digital x-ray more radiologists are using positive images (black objects on a white background). As art, both are acceptable, it is up to the artist and his client.

To produce a negative print–using traditional photographic means–one must reverse the original x-ray negative by copying it onto film. This can be be done either by making a contact print or by copying with a camera. Unfortunately, this method leads to some loss of sharpness. Using digital methods (PhotoShop or other imaging program) however, the image can be reversed without loss of detail.

I generally prefer positive images, especially for flowers. X-ray artists Conklin[1] and Veasey[2] generally use negative ones.

On the next few pages are examples of negative and positive prints of the same object. In the rest of the book the choice was up to the artist, but could easily be reversed if requested by the buyer.

OTHER X-RAY IMAGE MANIPULATIONS

Albert Richards[3] often used solarization or the Sabattier effect to enhance his images. In this method the print in the liquid developer is exposed to pure white light for a very brief time, producing a partial reversal. I have tried it but found the results too inconsistent to be practical. Now with digital methods one also can simulate the same effect in PhotoShop using the filter under Filter, then Stylize, then Solarize.

I often use a PhotoShop manipulation to produce what looks like a line drawing in the final image. The x-ray image is digitized at high resolution, opened in PhotoShop and under Filter, find Stylize, then Find Edges, the resulting image can then be manipulated to make it more or less contrasty and can then be used as a positive or negative.

Albert Richards[4] has also produced three dimensional x-ray images by stereoscopic means, but that technique requires most people to wear special eyeglasses, which are a nuisance and easily misplaced.

1. Conklin, William, Inner Dimensions, ISBN 1 56796-063 -4, WRS Publishing, 710 N, New Road, Waco, TX 76710
2. Veasey, Nick, http://www.nickveasey.com/
3. Richards, Albert G., The Secret Garden, ISBN 0-9628791-0-X, Almar Co., P.O. Box 15174, Ann Arbor, MI 48104
4. Richards, A., http://www-personal.umich.edu/~agrxray/3Dlily.html

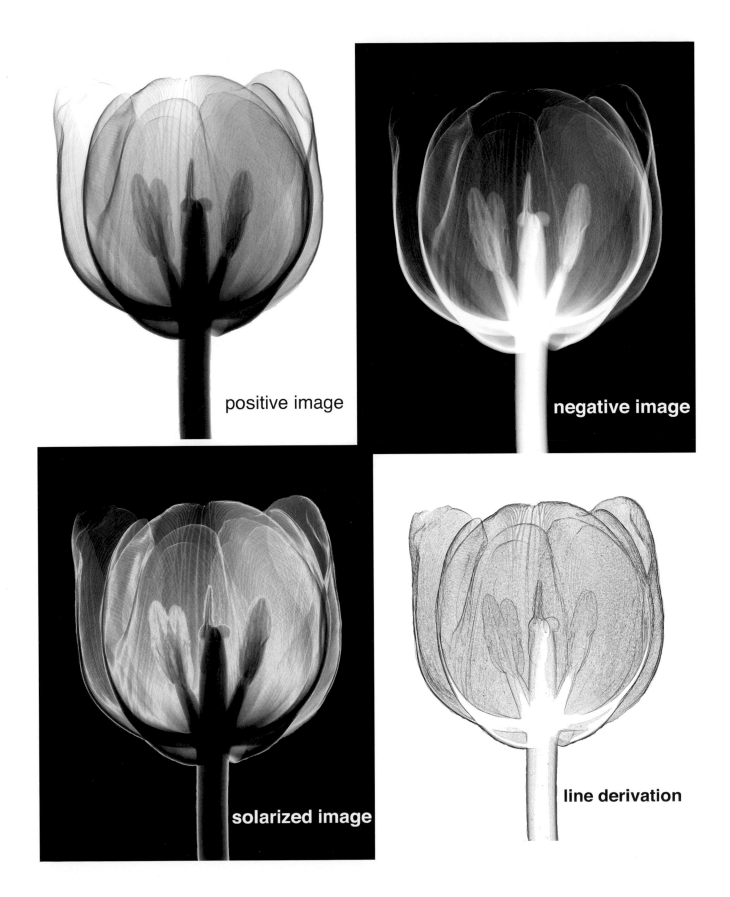

positive image

negative image

solarized image

line derivation

13

BLACK AND WHITE IMAGES

Chamberd Nautilis
Nautilus pompilus

15

Stargazer Lily Blossom
Lilium orientalis

Blue Crab
Callinectes sapidus

19

Tulip Blossom
Tulipa

21

Precious Wentletrap Shell
Epitonium angulatum

Orchid Blossom
Cattaleya labiata
Line Derivation

Snapdragon Blossom
Antirrhinum majus

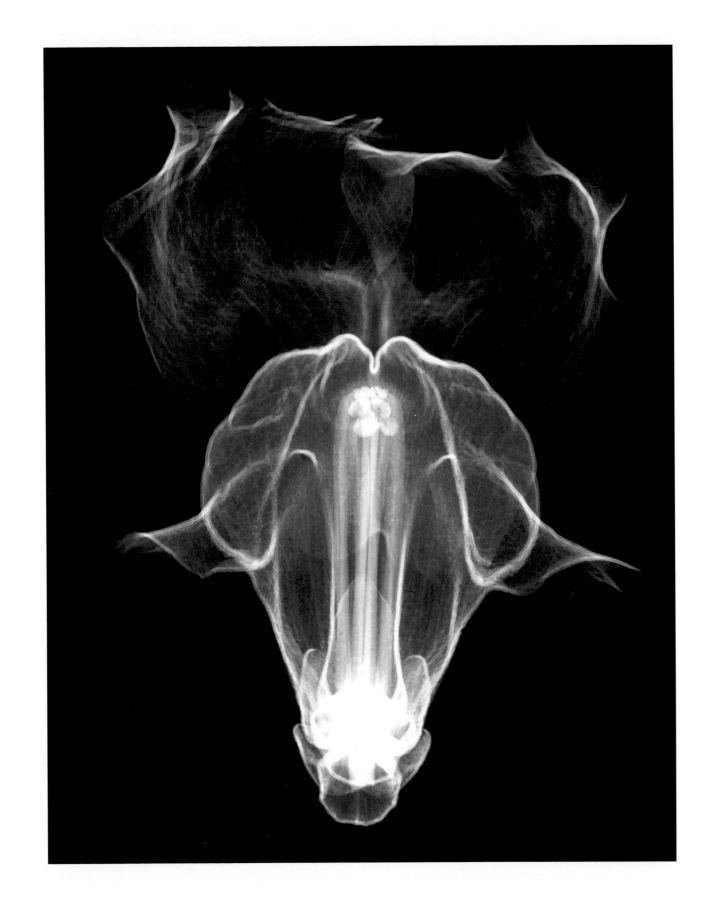

Florida Apple Shell
Pomacea paludosa

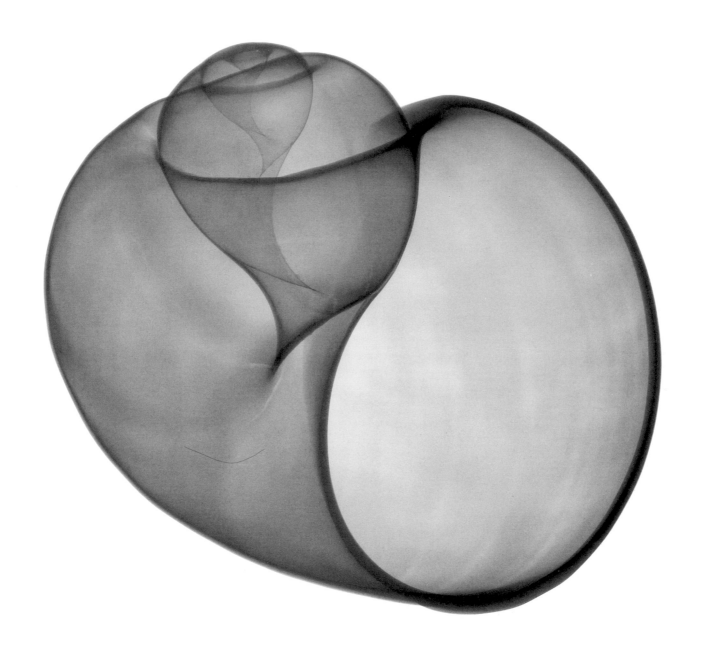

Pocket Calculator
Line Derivation

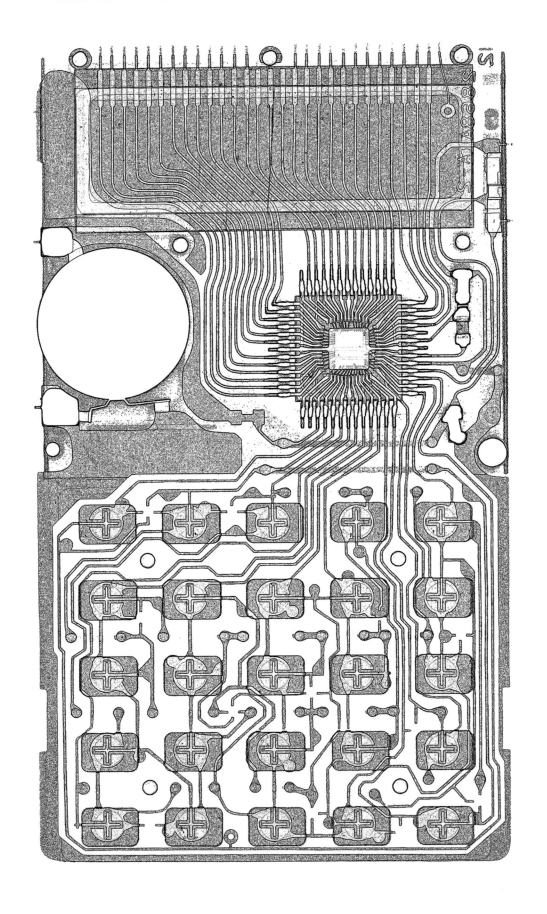

31

African Land Snail Shell
Achatina achatina

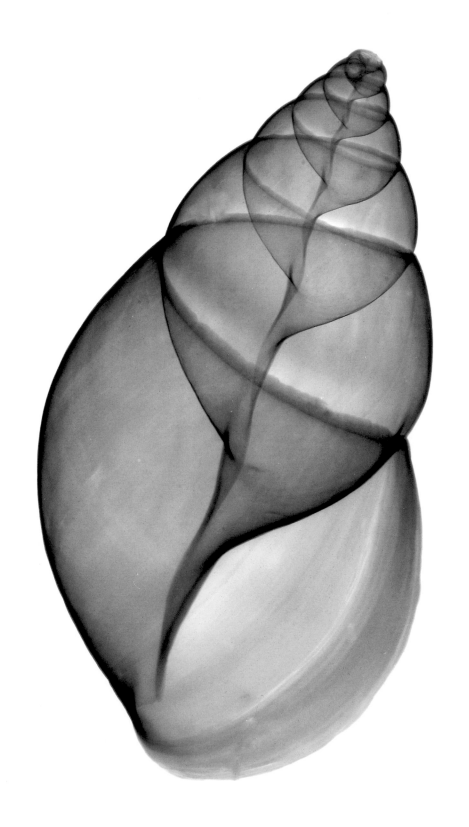

Partridge Tun Shell
Tonna perdix

34

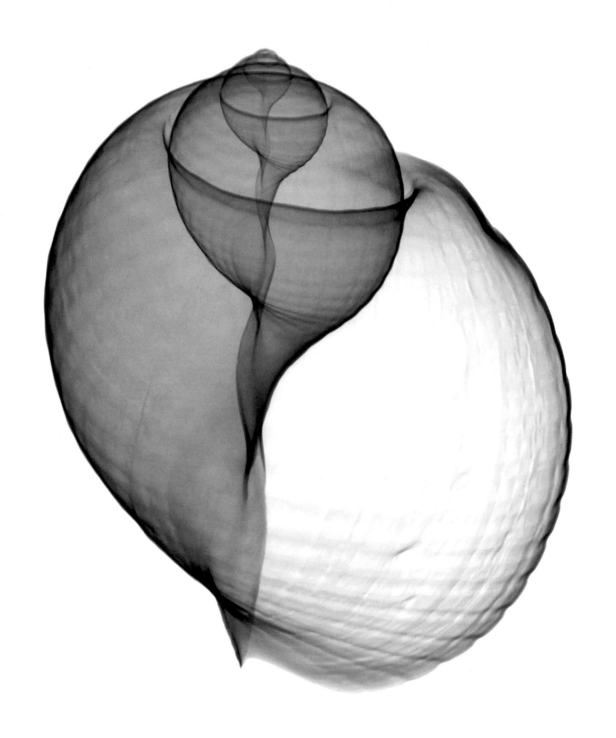

Pansy Blossom
Viola tricolor

Egg Cowery
Ovula ovum
Solarized Image

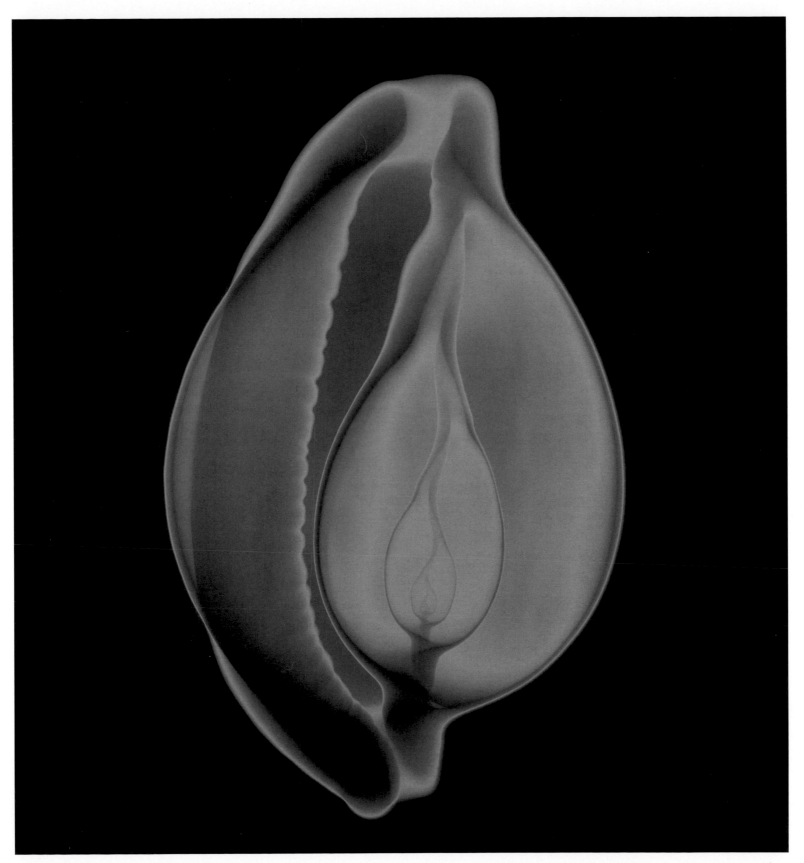

Golden Raintree Seed Pods
Koelreuteria paniculata

41

Angel Wing Clam Shells
Cyrtopleura costata

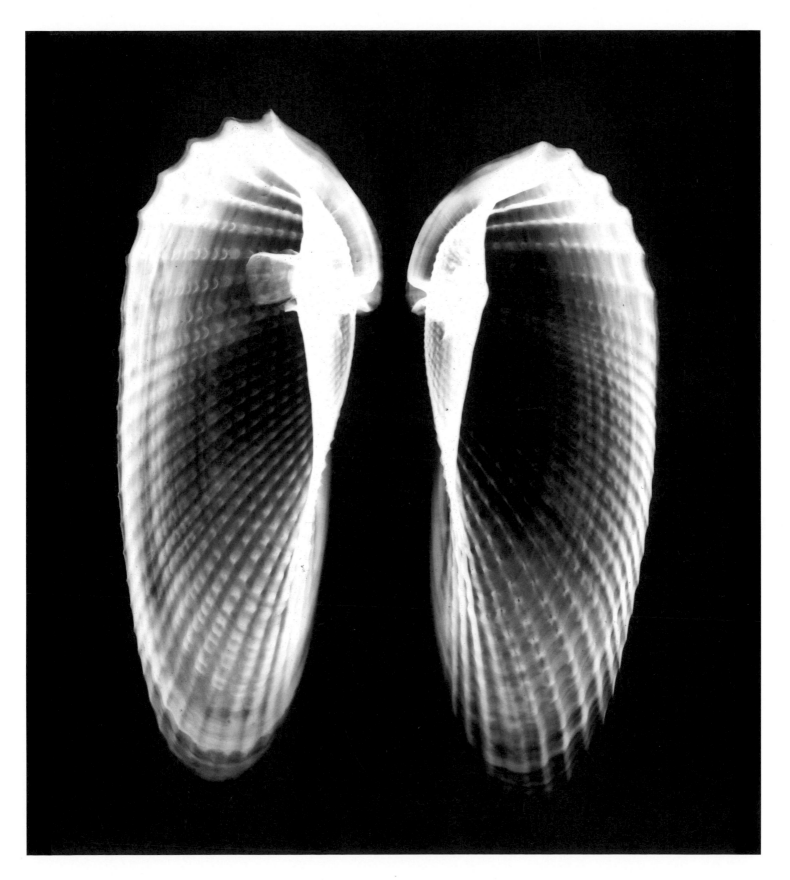

43

Starfish
Asteroidea
Line Derivation

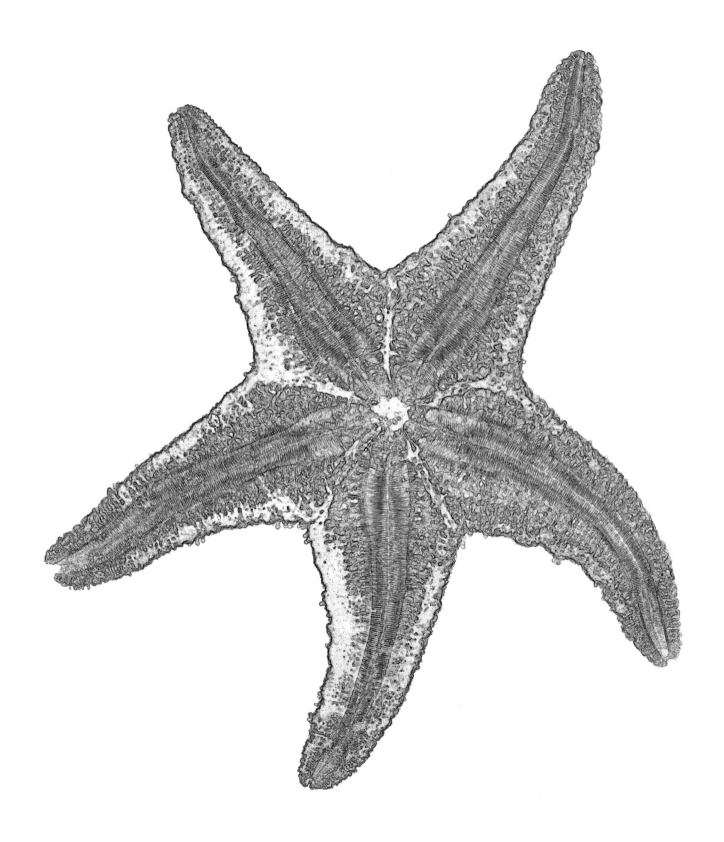

Trumpet Vine Blossom
Campsis grandiflora

Telescope Shell
Telescopium telescopium

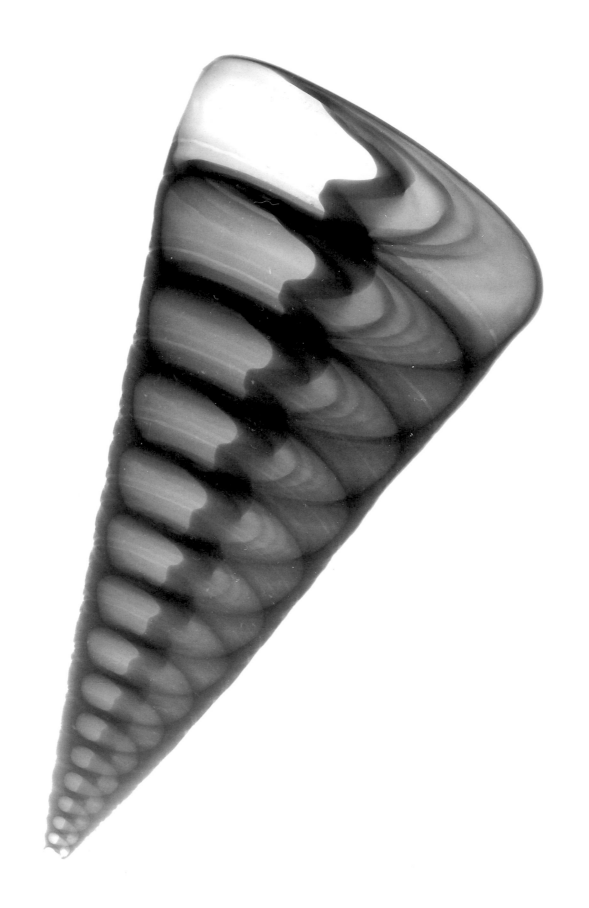

49

Guava Blossom
Psidium guajava

50

Banded Tun Shell
Tonna sulcosa

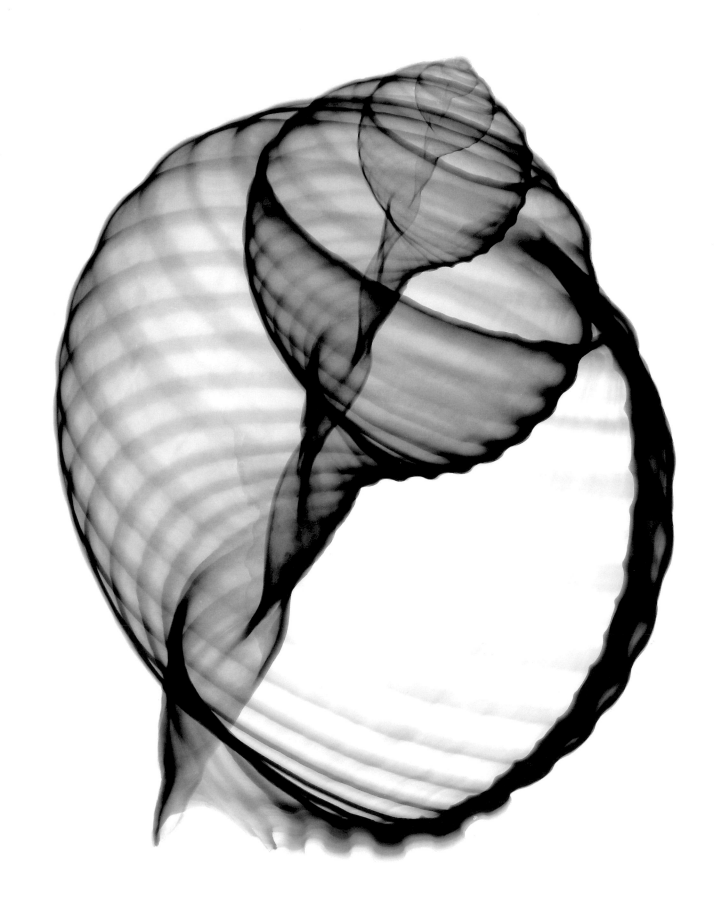

53

Pocket Watch

Lion's Paw Scallop
Nodipecten subnodosus
Solarized Image

Leaf of Celosia Plant
Cleosia cristata

Amaryllis Blossom
Hippeastrum

Sand Dollar
Echinarachnius parma

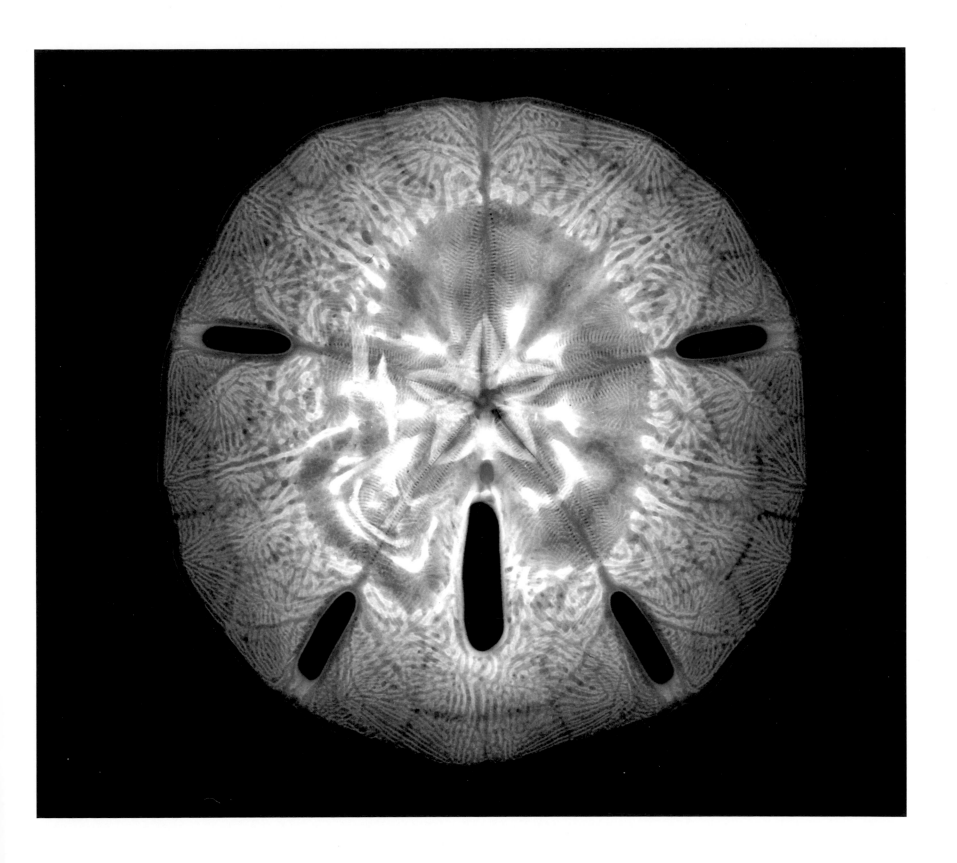

63

Sweetpea Blossoms
Lathyrus odoratus

65

Channeled Whelk Shell
Busycon canaliculatum

Sergeant Major Damselfish
Abudefduf saxatilis

Daffodil Blossom
Narcissus jonquilla

71

Harp Shell
Harpa articularis

Foxglove Blossoms
Digitalis purpurea

Leaf of Rice Paper Plant
Tetrapanax papyriferus

Atlantic Fig Shell
Ficus communis

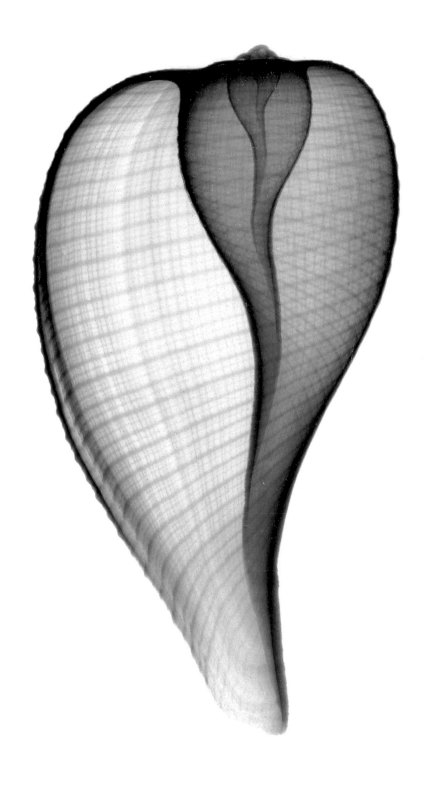

Horseshoe Crab
Limulus polyphemus

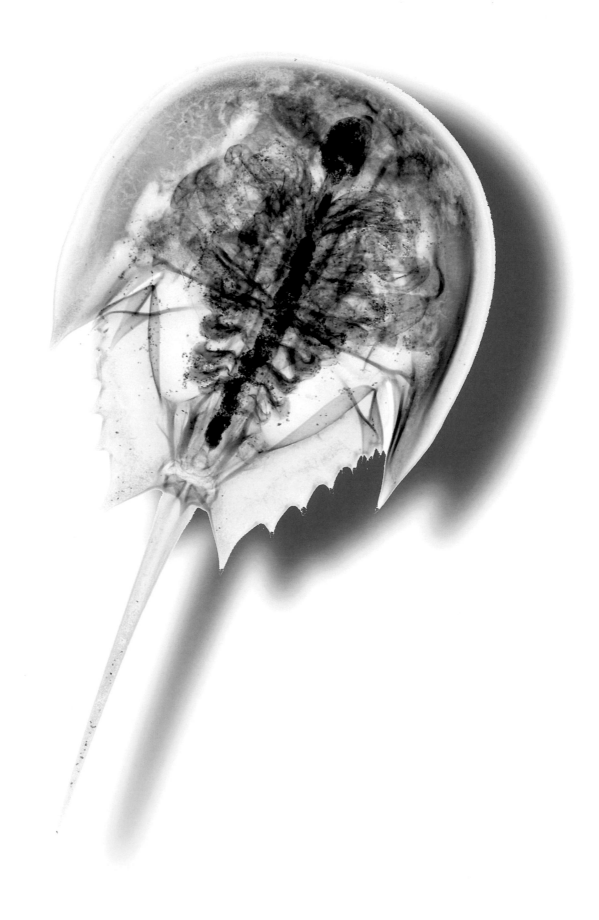

Umbrella Coral

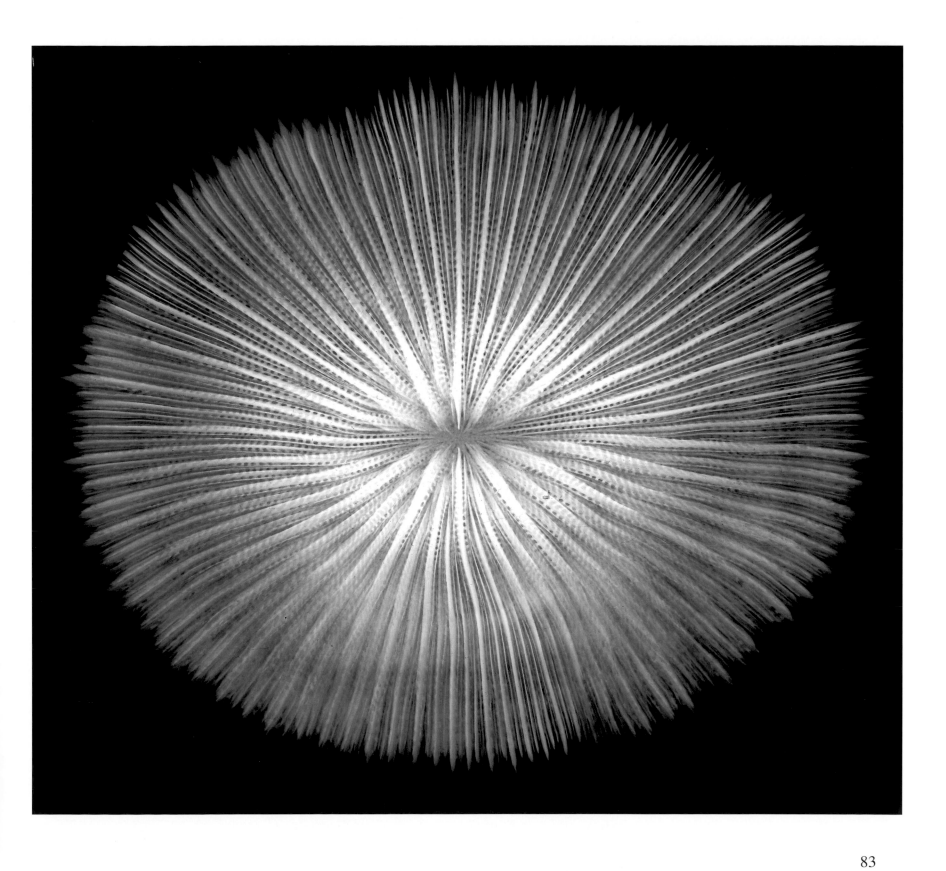

Fan Coral

85

Orchid
Phalalenopsis amabilis

87

Japanese Iris
Iris ensata

COLORED X-RAYS

All x-rays, whether captured on film, paper or a CCD are greyscale (B&W), but color can be added either in the darkroom or digitally.

The earliest methods of adding color to photographs was by toning, a chemical process in which the black silver image is bleached and then a faint color added by bathing the print in a chemical. The most common colors are brown (sepia) and blue, but just about any color can be achieved.

True and bright colors came much later – the first archival process was Cibachrome, and I made many images with this inconsistent and labor intensive process. The x-ray negative is placed in an enlarger, and color filters are put in the light beam exposing color sensitive papers such as Cibachrome or Kodacolor. This method is tedious and inconsistent, and even with great care in controlling time and temperature, no two prints look alike.

Fortunately newer digital methods are more predictable. The x-ray negatives or positive prints made from them are scanned at high resolution, then opened in an imaging editing program such as PhotoShop where color can be added with relative ease. For years the big problem with digital images was that stable prints were impossible to make. Now with better inks and papers, digital prints have the same archival qualities as any color prints, and are beginning to be accepted by museums and serious collectors.

Banded Tun Shell
Tonna sulcosa
Sepia Toned

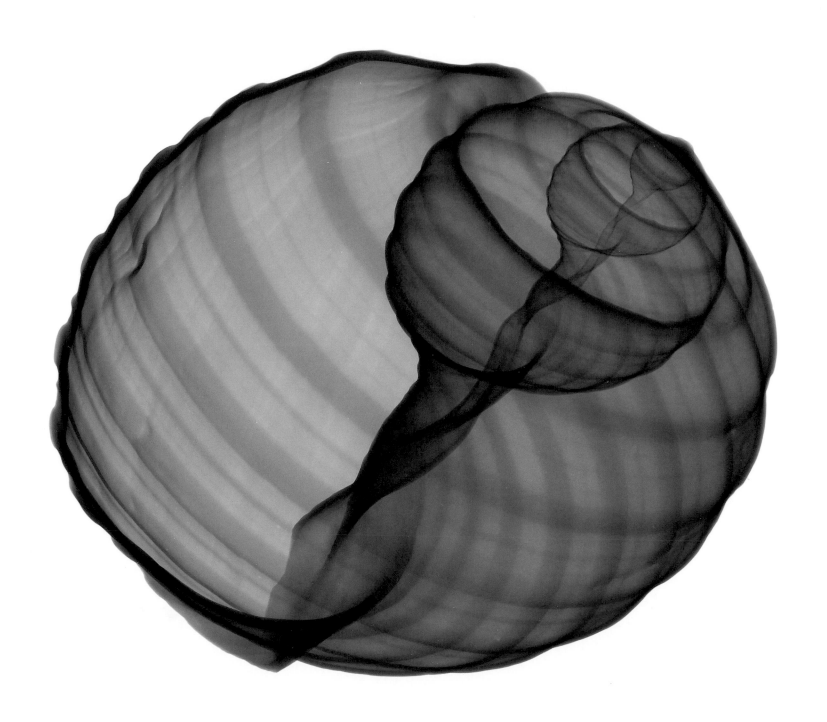

Calla Lilies
Zantedeschia aethopica

Leaves of Japanese Plum (Loquat) Tree
Eriobotrya japonica Lind

Generic Leaf

Martin's Tibia Shell
Tibia martinii
Blue Toned

99

Rose Blossom
Sepia Toned

Leaf of Gingko Tree
Gingko biloba

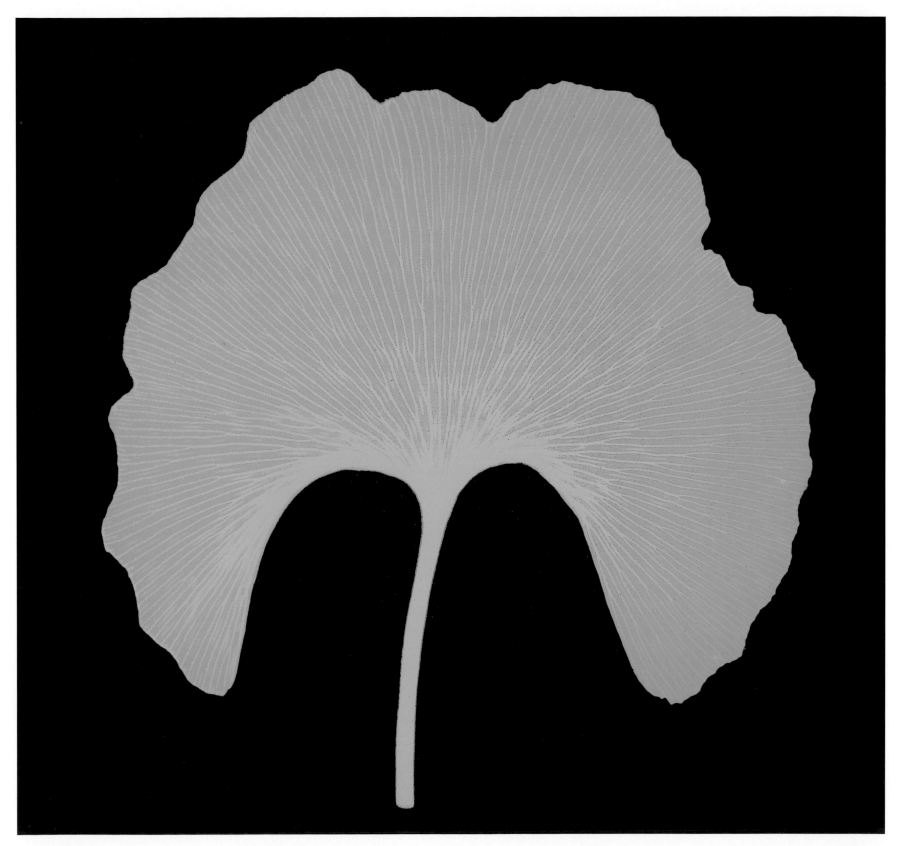

Amaryllis Blossom
Hippeastrum species

Japanese Iris Blossom
Iris ensata

107

MONTAGES

A montage is a grouping of two or more images presented as a unified whole. My earliest efforts were made by sandwiching two negatives in the enlarger, placing a photograph of a flower in the blank space at the center of an x-ray of the same flower. It was necessary to photograph the blossom on a black background on 4" X 5" sheet film, carefully adjusting the size of the image so it would fit in the clear area on the x-ray.

Then I began using multiple enlargers projecting several images onto the same sheet of paper. These techniques were perfected by Jerry Uelsmann[1], and my efforts included adding images from color slides to x-rays projected onto color paper (Cibachrome). This technique is very difficult and has been almost totally supplanted by image editing programs such as PhotoShop, in which multiple images can be combined with relative ease.

1. http://www.masters-of-photography.com/U/uelsmann/uelsmann.html

X-ray Negative

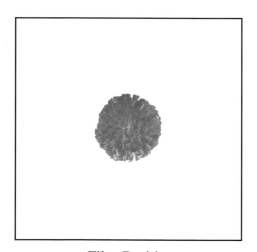

Film Positive

Sandwich

Plumeria Blossom
Plumeria rubra

Orchid Blossoms
Phalenopsis species

Precious Wentletrap Shells
Epitonium angulatum

113

Open Rose Pink

Ramshorn Snail Shell
Planorbis corneus

Checkerboard Bonnet Shell
Phalium areola

Star Shells
Guildfordia yoka

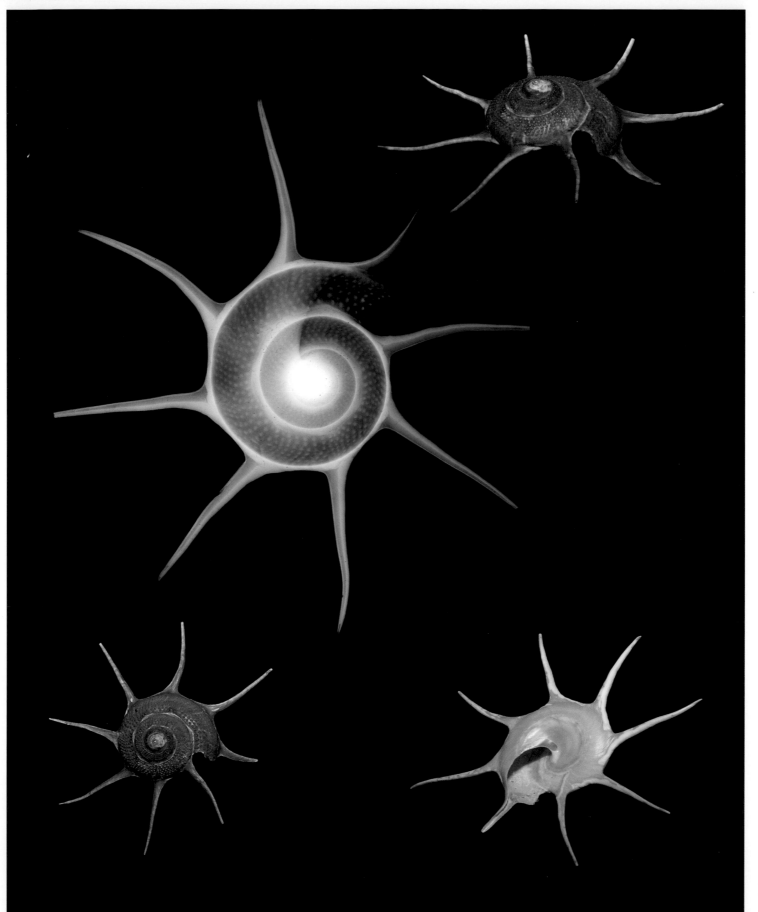

Pin Cushion Protea Blossoms
Leucospermium tottum

Venus Comb Murex Shells
Murex pecten

125

Emperor's Slit Shell
Mikadotrochus hirasei pilsbry 1903

Chambered Nautilus Shell
Nautilus pompilus

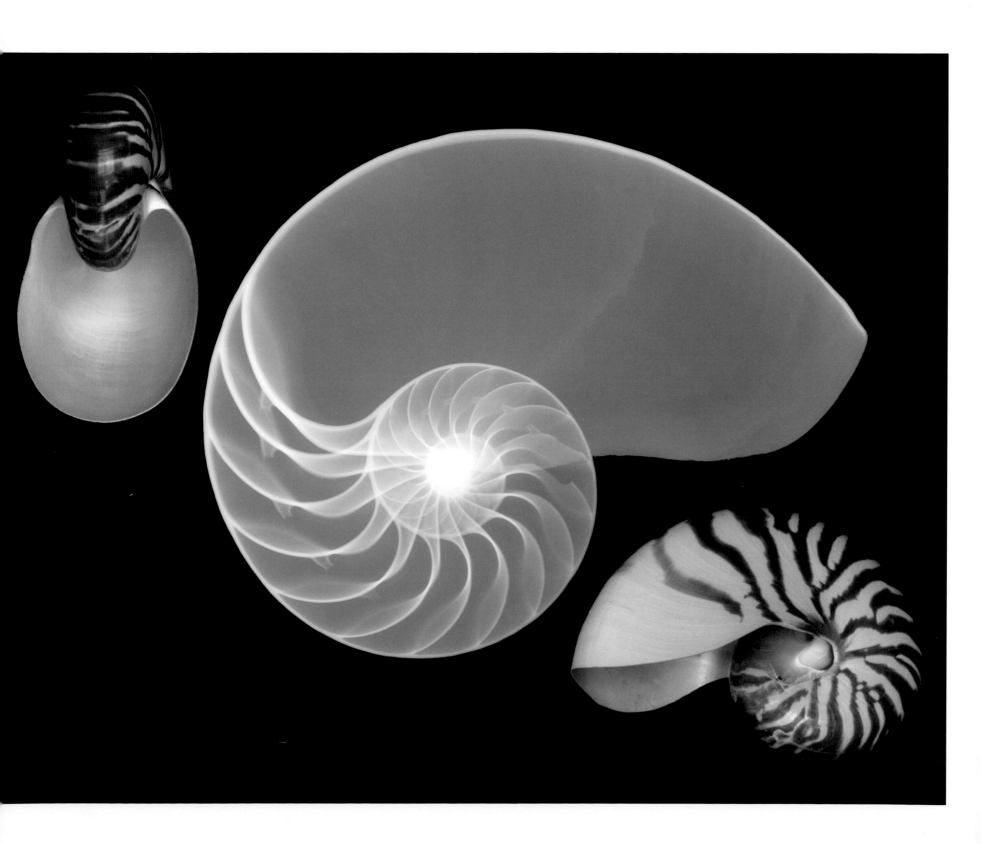

Daffodil
Narcissus jonquilla

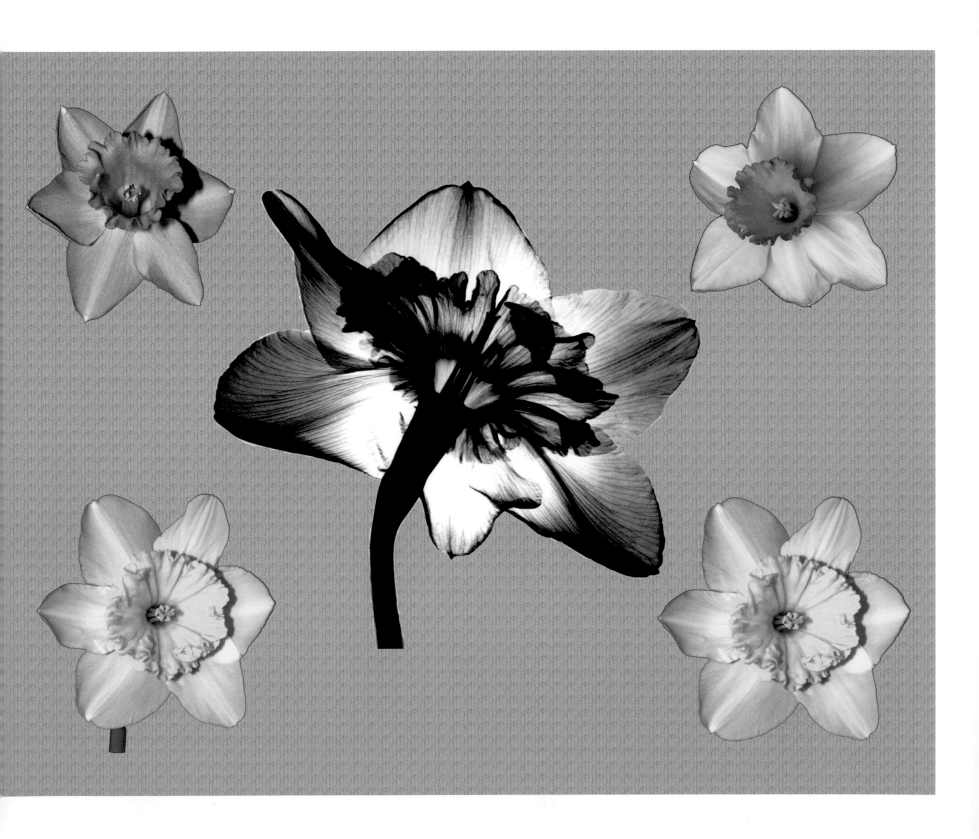

Frog Shell
Bursa perelegans

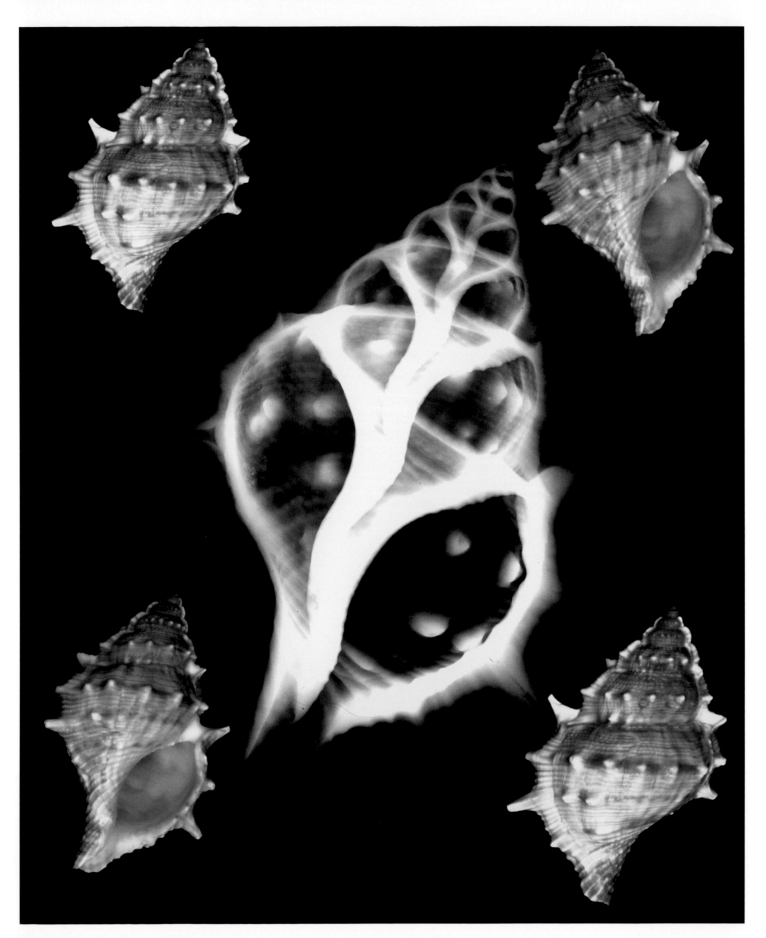

Martin's Tibia Shell
Tibia martinii

135

Open Rose Red

OTHER X-RAY ARTISTS

Although the first floral x-ray was made in 1914, the area has not attracted many artists, perhaps through fear of irradiation. Hopefully the publication of this book will encourage others to enter the field. With the technical information herein, any photographer with access to an x-ray machine should be able to produce comparable images. As of 2006, I know of only 12 other practitioners of the art. All of them were asked to submit one image to be used in this book. Those who responded have their image and contact info on the following pages.

WILLIAM CONKLIN

William Conklin is a native of South Carolina and a registered radiologic technologist. He made his first roentgenogram of a shell in 1976 after returning with many specimens from a trip to Sanibel Island in Florida. In 1978 he had a show of his images at the National Museum of Natural History of the Smithsonian Institution. He has published a book *"Inner Dimensions"* which combines color photographs with x-rays of the same shell.

He can be reached at:

William Conklin
Inner Dimension
1571 Marshall Ave.
Orangeburg, SC 29115
phone 803.534.8980

Editor's note12/17/06: I have heard that William Conklin died in 2006, but have been unable to verify it or find out if others would continue to make his prints.

DON DUDENBOSTEL

Don as born in Illinois, but moved to Oak Ridge, Tenn. in 1951, where his father worked as a design engineer. He attended the University of Tennessee, working his way as a photojournalist. He has been a commercial photographer since 1971. His interest in x-ray goes back a long way, when he assembled an Xray machine for a High school science project, and studied the effects of irradiation on growth of onions. He has been making art Xrays for 41 years, using both a Faxitron and a home made machine capable of 6 Kvp output.

He can be reached at:
Don Dudenbostel
11808 Rebel Pass
Knoxville, TN 37934
phone 865.809.2166
email: xrayarts@tds.net
http://x-rayarts.com/

143

ALBERT KOETSIER

Albert Koetsier was born in the Netherlands, and was educated as an electronic engineer at the technical university in Hilversum. He is self-educated in art history and photography. After graduating from college he began working for the x-ray division of Phillips medical systems. On a business trip to Wurtzberg, where Roentgen discovered x-rays, he saw a calender put out by Agfa which showed an x-ray images of flowers, and a new interest was born. He began working with x-rays as an art form in the 1970's, and continues to improve his technique and artistry. He has had shows of his work in Paris and numerous cities in the USA. He now lives in Southern California. More of his work can be seen at www.beyondlight.com and in Reader's Digest Nov. 2003 page 84.

He can be reached at:

Albert C. Koetsier
31721 St. Pierre Lane
Lake Elsinore CA 92530
phone 909.674.0207
fax 909.674.0599
email: ackoetsier@aol.com

JUDITH McMILLAN

Judith McMillan was trained as a teacher, but went back to art school to become a metal smith. Her life took a new direction when she took a photography course so that she could document her metal work. She fell in love with the camera and has never looked back. While photographing in the research collections at the Cleveland Museum of Natural History, she was offered the use of an x-ray machine. She has used the machine to image the internal structure of plant and insect material, revealing a world invisible to the human eye.

Her work may be seen at http://judithkmcmillan.com/
and prints can be purchased through:
Bonni Benrubi Gallery
41 East 57th Street, Suite 1300
New York, NY 10022
phone: 212-888-6007

She can be reached at:

Judith McMillan
Old Orchard
9044 Metcalf Rd.
Waite Hill, OH 44094
phone 440.256.8244

STEVEN N. MEYERS

Born in 1951 and a Native of Washington State, Currently working in the Seattle Area. My introduction to the photographic process began in 1971 when I began formal studies for radiological technology. I have made my living creating radiology-based images in the diagnostic medical setting for the last 30 years. It was this introduction the photographic process that lead to an interest in camera based photography in the late 70's. As a diversion from my daily world of black and white, I specialized in medium format color landscapes and nature photography, always making my own prints.

Around 1975, I began experimenting with making x-ray photographs of flowers and other objects mainly out of curiosity. These efforts were just for fun, but I kept the idea in the back of my mind to get serious about it someday. Well, before I knew it, 20 years had passed and the art form was almost forgotten. There have been a few other x-ray art photographers over the years, with the earliest floral radiographs made around 1914. The choice x-ray equipment for floral radiographs is almost as rare as the art form itself. Most medical diagnostic x-ray equipment is much too powerful for recording delicate flower details. I had previously saved a Published article on x-ray art by Bert Myers M.D in Diagnostic Imaging 1984 that gave me the proper direction for the best type of equipment to use. This article sat tucked away from 1984 to 1997.

In 1997 I became very serious about this art form and have created over 2000 different images since. Currently this collection is edited down to about 50 favorites, most of the images fail because of composition! There is no lens to compose the images. Floral radiography, even in its 70 year history, is for the most part unexplored, and I am committed to seeking out new and interesting subjects in nature.

Steve Meyers work can be seen at:
Portfolio at http://www.xray-art.com

149

MERRILL RAIKES

Merrill C. Raikes is an M.D. and a radiologist who practiced until 2000 when he retired from medicine and began taking art courses at a local college. He began x-raying flowers as a student project and his interest increased with time.

He can be reached at:

Merrill C. Raikes, M.D.
P.O. Box 810
Conway, MA 01341
704 Beldingville Road, Ashfield, MA 01330
phone 413.625.8352

SONNY RANDON

Sonny Randon was born in New Orleans in 1938. He is a third generation photographer. While his father was a commercial photographer who had a studio he sometimes worked in, his real interest in photography did not begin until he was in college.

The major portion of Randon's present business is color portraits and weddings, but his love is black and white scenics and portraits. His interest in x-ray images began after seeing a collection of them in a bookstore. He initially worked with Vincent Asaro, a friend who is a X-ray technician, but lacking the use of a low Kvp machine he was unable to obtain satisfactory images of flowers. He later associated with the author of this book, and now uses his Faxitron. He then scans the images into digital from and colors them in PhotoShop.

He can be reached at:
Sonny Randon Studio
1900 Veterans Blvd.
Metarie, LA 70005
phone 504.837.1236
www.sonnyrandon.com

152

153

ALBERT RICHARDS

Albert G. Richard's training in photography began at an early age from his father, a professional photographer. He earned academic degrees in Chemical Engineering and Physics at the University of Michigan. In 1940 he joined the University of Michigan School of Dentistry as an instructor and focused his interest on x-ray photography and its application to dentistry by teaching himself dental radiography. Among Richards' accomplishments is the invention of the recessed cone x-ray head; he was the first to use the electron microscope to view the internal microstructure of teeth; and he devised a liquid mold technique for showing the topography of surfaces, which has had diverse applications in other fields, e.g., in determining fingerprints of burn victims. Other inventions of his include Dynamic Tomography, a radiographic procedure that allows physicians and dentists to examine living tissue layer by layer, and the Buccal Object Rule, a method for determining the relative location of objects hidden in the oral cavity. He holds six patents on his inventions.

In addition to x-raying teeth during his long career, Professor Richards' curiosity led him to radiograph a vast range of objects which included bombs, bird wings, insects, metal castings, tadpoles, fossils, skulls, knives, ancient artifacts, animals, pollen grains, snow flakes, wood panels and flowers. He found radiographing flowers to be both technically challenging and esthetically rewarding. One afternoon in 1960, he made a modest purchase that marked a turning point in his life. He bought a bunch of daffodils for twenty-seven cents, took them to the dental school, and made his first 2-D floral radiograph. That image wasn't very satisfactory to him, however the potential for developing techniques for making high quality images of flowers piqued his interest. That interest became a passion to which he devoted all of his time following retirement from the University of Michigan in 1981. His collection of 2-D and 3-D floral radiographs exceeds 3700 images. When slides of his 3-D images are projected onto a silver screen and viewed through Polaroid glasses, the observer sees the blossoms in their natural rounded form.

Professor Richards' floral radiographs were first published in 1962 in the National Geographic's School Bulletin, and since then have appeared in textbooks, calendars, encyclopedias, museums and many magazines in this country as well as Italy, India, Germany, Japan and the Soviet Union. He is the author of more than 100 publications including a book, "The Secret Garden — 100 x-rays of Flowers" (1990). The October 1986 issue of the Smithsonian Magazine featured his floral x-rays on the front cover and on five interior pages. In 1990 Smithsonian Press published a beautiful book called "Editor's Choice Smithsonian." The senior editor surveyed the 2000 articles that had appeared in the Smithsonian Magazine in the 20 years since its beginning and chose his favorite 37 articles for this anniversary book. Professor Richards' article was one of them.

Professor Richards' collection has become
Richards' Radiographs, LLC and can be seen at:
http://www-personal.umich.edu/~agrxray/gallery.html

155

HUGH TURVEY

Hugh Turvey is a London based photographer and artist. He trained as a designer and art director but soon discovered photography offered more creative freedom and working independence. 1996 saw his move into x-ray/shadow photography when he was asked to produce an album cover image of broken bones. With a newfound interest in x-ray he produced an extensive series of x-ray images of every day objects (with the backing of the Science Photo Library, London) that was finally published on the 4 April 1999 in *The Observer Magazine* (LIFE) in the U.K. The article generated interest that has snow-balled an x-ray photography career to date and saw the launch of GUSTO, a company set up by Hugh Turvey and Artemi Kyriacou to produce photography and x-ray imagery for clients throughout Europe and occasionally America.

He can be reached at:

GUSTO | Hugh Turvey
1 Caversham Lodge
95 Grove Ave.
London, N10 2AJ, U.K.
phone 44 20 8442 1499
email: email@xrayartist.com
www.gustoimages.com

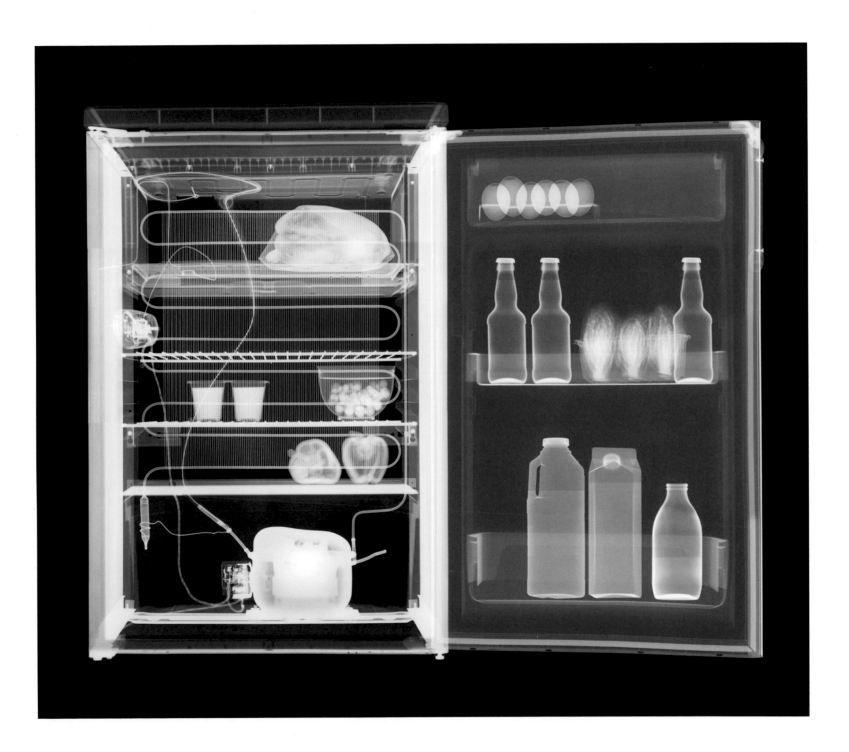

NICK VEASEY

Nick Veasey was born in the United Kingdom and had no formal training in any discipline. He has worked for Reuters and in the advertising and travel businesses. He learned photography on his own. Since 1995, he has devoted himself full time to photography, specializing in x-ray, scientific, and abstract images..

He first got into x-ray when he unsuccessfully tried to win a contest to discover what was inside a sealed soda can.

He has made remarkable x-ray images of large objects such as refrigerators, automobiles, and other machines.

Those wishing to see more of Nick Veasey's work should visit:
http://www.nickveasey.com/nickveasey.html

He can be reached at:

Radar Studio
Coldblow Lane
Thurnam
Maidstone
Kent ME14 3LR
United Kingdom
phone 44 0 1622 737722
email: nick@nickveasey.com

INDEX OF IMAGES AND ARTISTS